Moments with Dad:
A Devotional Memoir

Kelly L. Valencia-Aiken

MOMENTS WITH DAD: A DEVOTIONAL MEMOIR
PUBLISHED BY KLVA PUBLISHING
Colorado Springs, CO, 80916
LittleMsWordsmith@gmail.com

ISBN: 1517542154
ISBN-13: 978-1517542153

Printed in the United States of America

DEDICATION

This book is written for and dedicated to my superhero, my dad, James Larry Mitchell. I love you, Daddy. I'm so thankful for and so very proud of you. You are such a wonderful dad and have taught me so much. You are living a legacy you will leave to your children and grandchildren and I am so honored to be your daughter. I am privileged to be a faith partner with you, believing together with you for the fullness of God's glory to be manifested in your life. I am so looking forward to watching the plans of God unfold in your life and watching you go from faith to faith and glory to glory as you walk out your destiny in Christ! I'm so blessed to have you as my dad. I love you so incredibly much, Daddy! I wish you the happiest 60th birthday, Daddy! May the next sixty years be your best years yet, in Jesus' name!!!

CONTENTS

ACKNOWLEDGEMENTS

I thank the Lord for giving me the idea and helping me to write this book for my dad. It would never have happened without His divine inspiration or the support of my incredible husband, Robert, whom I love and adore so very much! Honey, thank you for all you do: all the help with the kids, the house, the encouragement, and the support you give me. You're such a precious, priceless blessing! I truly cherish you and the wonderful marriage we have together. I thank God for you, my Love! I want to give special thanks to Kimberly Bauer for proofing and editing this book, and also to my mom, brothers, and friends Alena Tvrznik, Alycia Stiltner, Elise Forte, Hannah Bartholomew, Pastors Garry and Martha Beecher, and Toni Haynes, who prayed for and helped finalize this project. You are all such a blessing to me and I'm so thankful for you!

DAY ONE

"For the LORD God is a sun and shield: the LORD will give grace and glory: no good thing will he withhold from them that walk uprightly" (Psalm 84:11).

I grew up listening to my dad shred on the guitar. I loved just sitting there listening to him play for hours at a time. My all-time favorite song to hear him play – and the one he played most often – was "House of the Rising Sun." He never sang the lyrics. He didn't have to. He would rock back and forth, head swaying, his face telling the story as he played. I imagined the song to be a mournful, lamenting song. It turns out I was pretty spot on when, years later, I actually read the lyrics. Now, although the place down in New Orleans didn't sound very inviting, I sure did love watching my dad come alive with every strum of that electric guitar. It was his passion.

Today, that passion is paving the road for my father to become a multi-billionaire with the musical inventions he's created. He has been gifted by God to take something he loves and create something new, something exciting, something that has never existed before and is taking the music industry by storm. It's God's grace on my dad's life enabling him to answer musical problems with ingenious inventions. It's God's glory – His goodness – on my dad's life that promotes and positions him with great wealth, the right connections, the right resources, and gives him divine appointments, as well as divine avoidances, that push him forward into his destiny.

That's just how God works: He desires to bestow His goodness upon us and watch us live the life He planned for us to enjoy. Just as we physically need time in the sun's light to absorb nutrients properly for survival, we need time in the Son's light to grow, mature, and develop the way we were designed. The more time we spend with Him, the more He is able to shed light on our path, showing us how to achieve our purpose and live a fulfilling life. Spend time today in His presence and be on the lookout for manifestations of His goodness.

Today, I will expect the Lord to light my path and keep me from all harm. His grace is my strength and He is my glory. His goodness is poured out upon me and every good gift is added unto me because I am in right-standing with Him through Jesus.

DAY TWO

"Therefore if any man be in Christ, he is a new creature: old things are passed away; behold, all things are become new" (2 Corinthians 5:17).

There are five syllables that bring a smile to my dad's face and a pep in his step quicker than any other words or phrases I know - "Salvation Army." Second to that would be "garage sale." My dad is a very enthusiastic secondhand store shopper. He can literally spend hours – an entire day, even! – walking around a Salvation Army store admiring the vast and often random collections of people's former belongings. There is something so true about the phrase, "One man's junk, another man's treasure."

Just as my dad loves finding hidden "treasures" among the resale items cluttering the shelves of many a thrift store, God loves to find hidden treasures among those whom the world considers to be junk, trash, worthless, those who have been forgotten, abandoned, neglected, rejected, and often discarded by society. In fact, God is supreme at taking what someone else has thrown away and making it brand new.

His Word says in 2 Corinthians 5:17 that when we come to Him and give our lives to Him, He makes us new. He completely transforms every part of our spiritual being so that we are an entirely new creation in Christ Jesus. He takes all of the sin nature that once

3

separated us from Him and removes it as far as the east is from the west (Psalm 103:12). As any good resale shopper would repurpose a formerly used and abused object, Jesus gives renewed purpose to the lives of people who surrender to Him. Salvation Army was, after all, His idea.

Today, I will surrender my brokenness to the Lord and allow Him to bring new purpose and meaning to those areas of my life.

DAY THREE

"Husbands, love your wives, even as Christ also loved the church, and gave himself for it; that he might sanctify and cleanse it with the washing of water by the word" (Ephesians 5:25-26).

"We're going to the car wash, car wash!" Sung by a swooning guy in his thirties and a young girl of about six years of age, this is a very fun and exciting song to sing! I loved singing with my dad and this was a song we both enjoyed as we were on our way to wash the car. It was an adventure watching the car get soaped up and washed clean. My favorite part was when the car passed through the mitter curtain – those long, soft strips of cloth hanging from a motorized shaft that gently wiped the car from front to back as the car rolled down the track. The foam applicator and the large scrubbers at each side of the car were tons of fun to watch, too, as they made a slapping sound on the windows and doors. The part I was never too certain of, however, was at the end. The big, loud dryer looked and sounded like it was going to crash right through the windshield, but it never did. It would touch down on little rollers and blast away beads of water with its breath. It was powerful, but somehow gentle enough to finish the car wash without damaging the vehicle.

As our Heavenly husband, that is exactly what Jesus is like. He is all-powerful, yet gentle in His strength. He takes us in all of our dirtiness with the shame of our past, our bad habits, the thoughts we shouldn't be thinking, and He begins to gently and carefully wipe off the dirt and wash us clean through His Word. That is how we also should treat one another in the Body of Christ, patiently and lovingly looking past the dirt and using the Word to restore people to beauty once again. The more we meet with Him in the quiet places we are able, as a vehicle in an automated car wash tunnel, to get on track with the cleansing work He's doing in our lives. That's how He loves us! We are dirty and broken when we come to Him, yet in His great love for us, He keeps washing us through His Word until we are clean and made whole again.

Today, I will allow the Lord Jesus to point out the areas in my heart and life that need His cleansing touch and to wash me with His Word.

DAY FOUR

"Thy word have I hid in mine heart, that I might not sin against thee" (Psalm 119:11).

Concentration. That was our favorite game to play. The memory-building, recall-challenging game of picture matching was always a blast to play with my dad. He wasn't one of those dads who would always lose to his kid, either. He played to win! He would line up those little squares and give me the "game on" look that said he was serious about beating me. He taught me how to be a good sport when it came to losing. And it didn't take me long to learn how to memorize and remember quickly so I had a prayer of a chance of winning!

My dad didn't just teach me to remember pictures in a game, though. He taught me how to memorize the Word of God. I grew up learning Bible verses in church for Sunday school, but the first real challenge to learn the Scriptures came from my dad. He dared utter the defying words, "I'll bet you can't memorize this passage by the end of the week," as he pointed to Psalm 23. He certainly knew how to motivate me. I had the scripture committed to heart by the very next morning and I have never forgotten it since!

Memorizing the Word isn't just a great thing to do to prove to someone you can; it's something that changes and can save your life. The Word of God transforms you from the inside out, keeps you from living a life of sin, and is ever-ready for use in times of trouble when your Bible is nowhere nearby. There have been moments in my life when the only word I could say in the situation was, "Jesus!" In many other situations, I have been victorious because I had the Word of God in my heart, ready to be pulled out and put to use as a sword against the enemy in times of temptation or trial. You don't have to start with learning entire chapters at a time - a simple verse will do. Begin today with a renewed commitment to memorize the Word of God. Your life will never be the same.

Today, I will put God's Word in front of my eyes, in my ears, in my heart, and in my mouth so His Word becomes a part of my innermost being.

DAY FIVE

"Death and life are in the power of the tongue: and they that love it shall eat the fruit thereof" (Proverbs 18:21).

"Once upon a time, in a land far away, there was a hill." All of my dad's stories began with a hill. Something magical, mysterious, or even sometimes spooky, was at the top of that hill. We played a game where one of us would begin a story – his with the introduction of the infamous hill – and the other person would add to it, taking turns until some outlandish tale had been told that made us both laugh. We came up with some pretty wild stories. In hindsight, we could have written some very unique children's books! It was a lot of fun sharing and using our imaginations together.

Just like my dad and I would spend time creating and using our imaginations together, the Lord invites us to do the same with Him. Jesus said in Mark 11:23 that we can have whatsoever we say. Whatever we say! He also gives us a warning that whatever is in our hearts will ultimately end up on our lips (Luke 6:45). It is important to have our minds renewed as we are commanded in Romans 12:2 in order for our hearts to believe and store up good things for our mouths to proclaim.

My dad's favorite book is all about proclamation. "The Tongue: A Creative Force" by Charles Capps has been handed out to every member of our family and even to several friends. In it the author describes using your mouth to speak what you want over your life: the promises of God, the healing that belongs to you, the prosperity you haven't tapped into yet that is on its way, etc. He explains we are the prophets of our own lives. We have the unique, God-given ability to use our imaginations, line them up with the character and Word of God, and begin to speak out the life we desire. Now is the time to stop professing the reality we don't want to continue in and start telling the God-story of our lives!

Today, I will use my faith-based imagination to speak words of life over myself, as well as the people and situations in my life.

DAY SIX

"And hath raised us up together, and made us sit together in heavenly places in Christ Jesus" (Ephesians 2:6).

One of the most important things you can teach a child is where s/he lives, their phone number, and how to contact emergency services. I still remember jumping up and down on my dad's bed as he made learning where I live into a fun game. He must have spent a good hour or more having me recite to him my address, home phone, and the ever-important "911" number.

"What's your address?" He'd ask.

"48818 Salt River Road, New Baltimore, Michigan, 48047," I'd answer as I bounced.

"Good! What's your phone number?"

I'd laugh and say, "That's easy! It's 810-725-0521!"

"Now, who do we call in the case of emergencies?"

"9-1-1!" I'd shout back, still jumping on the bed, pigtails flying as my dad grinned at me for a job well done.

Just like it's vital for a young child to know where they live in case they get lost, we as Christians need to know where *we* are located in case *we* get lost! Ephesians 2:6 says in the NIV, "And God raised us up with Christ and seated us with him in the heavenly realms in Christ Jesus." Though we live in a physical world on Earth, we are spiritually positioned in the heavens in Christ Jesus. To understand the full implication of what it means to be placed where we are spiritually, let's take a look at Ephesians 1:20-23: "…He raised him from the dead, and set him at his own right hand in the heavenly places, far above all principality, and power, and might, and dominion, and every name that is named, not only in this world, but also in that which is to come: and hath put all things under his feet, and gave him to be the head over all things to the church, which is his body, the fullness of him that filleth all in all." Seated together with Him and in Him means that we, too, are located far above all principalities, powers, rulers, authorities, leaders, or any other form of might and dominion – over everything named! – in this world and the one to come. That is some serious authority!

We have authority through Jesus over EVERY name: cancer, diabetes, strife, poverty, lack, stress, demons, and so on. Anything that would come against us has to bow to the name of Jesus. We exercise that right legally because we are seated in a position of power, resting in the finished work of Jesus. When the enemy tries to tell you that you have no power over him, remember location, location, location! Regardless of the tactic the enemy tries to use against us we are **already** positioned to overcome because we are seated *with* Jesus and *in* Jesus. He is the head of the Church and we are His Body. If all things have been put under His feet, as the Body of Christ, they are under *our* feet, as well! Don't let the enemy walk all over you. Trample him underfoot!

Today, I will rest in my position in Christ Jesus in authority over all principalities, powers, and demonic entities because of His finished work on the cross. The devil is under my feet and everything he tries to bring against me must bow to the name of Jesus!

DAY SEVEN

"Finally, my brethren, be strong in the Lord, and in the power of his might. Put on the whole armor of God, that ye may be able to stand against the wiles of the devil" (Ephesians 6:10-11).

"Pretend they just killed your dog." Those were fighting words – literally. That's what my dad told me to imagine as I went to karate to spar with my classmates. I took those words to heart and fought with every ounce of rage in me, picturing my black lab, Candy, being slaughtered at the heartless hands of whoever was the unlucky one picked to fight me in that match. Growling, I punched and kicked and chased the other person across the room with as much force as I could muster. Unfortunately, my sensei, Brian Toso, who, without protective gear, just happened to move into the line of my sweeping roundhouse kick at the exact moment my opponent stepped backward. He got the full force of my kick right between his legs. He doubled over, groaning, but I just kept mercilessly pounding on my sparring partner until my sensei recovered enough to call the match. I was, after all, fighting the person who murdered my dog!

That is how we are to treat the enemy of our souls - as the murderer he is! The Lord Jesus said in John 10:10, "The thief cometh not, but for to steal, and to kill, and to destroy: I am come that they might have life, and that they might have it more abundantly." We are not to think lightly of our adversary. He is out to steal, kill, and destroy. We must know how to skillfully use the sword of the Spirit to punch and kick and chase him right out of our lives with the Word of God. We cannot war against the enemy in our own strength and wisdom. Ephesians 6:11 says that the devil has "wiles" or strategies. Only when we are strong in the Lord and in *His* power, in *His* might, are we able to effectively fight the evil one.

Like I would fight against my classmates, we need to combat the enemy. To spar in NAAMA (North American Association of Martial Arts) karate, you were required to wear padding. I had a helmet, a mouth guard, a padded vest, forearm and shin guards, special padded shoes, and gloves. If the other person had not been wearing the same protective gear, just that outfit alone would have been enough to scare them off! Just as I was bedecked from head to toe in padding, we need to be clothed from head to toe in our battles with the devil. We need to have on our belt of truth, the breastplate of righteousness, shoes of peace, shield of faith, helmet of salvation, the sword of the spirit, and the lance of intercession. Only when we are properly dressed and operating in the power of His might will we be able to "stand and keep on standing" our ground in the fight of faith.

Today, I will put on the full armor of God. I am strong in the Lord and the power of His might, able to stand against the wiles of the devil.

DAY EIGHT

"Finally, brethren, whatsoever things are true, whatsoever things are honest, whatsoever things are just, whatsoever things are pure, whatsoever things are lovely, whatsoever things are of good report; if there be any virtue, and if there be any praise, think on these things" (Philippians 4:8).

One of the fun things I got to do as a kid growing up was to shoot things. I don't mean that I went hunting – I probably would've cried if I saw something killed. I enjoyed shooting things like pop bottles, bricks, cans, and other targets. My dad and my uncle, his brother, bought some guns, as well as a bow and arrow, and taught my three younger brothers and me how to use them. At first when we all tried, we were WAY off with our aim. To say that we could not have hit the broad side of a barn was an understatement. After a while, we learned to use the scope on the guns and to line up the arrow in such a way that both bullets and arrows began to hit their target.

The Word of God tells us we have a target we should always be focusing on with our minds: we need to fix our minds on and think about things that are true, honest, just, pure, lovely, of a good report, virtuous, and praiseworthy. At first, you may find your thoughts wandering all over the place. More often than not, you may "miss the mark" in trying to control your thoughts. The good news is, the more you are in the Word of God and make an effort to be aware of the thoughts and feelings you're experiencing, the more you are able to control them. You can, through time and practice, become an excellent marksman of the mind by learning to, with laser-like focus, reject thoughts and emotions that don't meet the criteria above. When something enters your mind that falls short of the target, dismiss it immediately. This is something you must do intentionally.

Second Corinthians 10:3-5 tells us how to be intentional in our thinking. "For though we walk in the flesh, we do not war after the flesh: (For the weapons of our warfare are not carnal, but mighty through God to the pulling down of strong holds;) casting down imaginations, and every high thing that exalteth itself against the knowledge of God, and bringing into captivity every thought to the obedience of Christ." Our spiritual battleground is not a physical place somewhere. We do battle with the enemy mostly in our own minds, resisting the lies he whispers in our ears that masquerade as our own thoughts. When we purpose to pay attention to what we are thinking, we are able to make a conscious decision about those thoughts and to cast them down, refuse them, and refute them with the Word of God when they do not line up to His standards.

Today, I will take heed to what I am thinking and focus my thoughts on God's best for me, those things that are true, honest, just, pure, lovely, of a good report, virtuous, and praiseworthy. I will take hold of every thought that is contrary to His standards and cast them down, replacing them with the truth of the Word of God.

DAY NINE

"The Lord shall fight for you, and ye shall hold your peace." (Exodus 14:14).

When I was in my senior year of high school, my mom had carpal tunnel surgery done on her right wrist. She was grossed out at the thought of cleaning the wound. That sort of thing didn't bother me, so I offered to help and uttered a sentence that changed the course of my life: "I'll clean it for you. It'll be training for the nurse I'll never be." Faster than I could blink, both my parents were set on me becoming a nurse. My dad spent hours praying I would be admitted into nursing school. He even went to the principal and my counselor and fought hard to gain permission for me to become dually enrolled in college while finishing high school. They agreed to let me attend college as long as I checked in for attendance purposes three days a week. And, just like that, I was accepted into nursing school and began attending college classes before I graduated from high school.

Just like my dad fought on my behalf for my education, God fights for us, as well. There are moments in our walks with Him when He sends us into battle and gives us the strategies to overcome and emerge triumphantly. There are other times when He says, "You won't have to fight this battle. I've got this. Be still and watch Me deliver you" (2 Chronicles 20:17, *paraphrased*). Exodus 15:3 says, "The

Lord is a warrior; the Lord is his name." He is well able to fight on your behalf in whatever situation you are facing and bring you the victory. What are the faith-battles you are facing today? Take time to be still and hear from the Lord His plan to get you through triumphantly.

Today, I will put my trust in the Lord and allow Him to fight on my behalf while I remain in perfect peace.

DAY TEN

"Have not I commanded thee? Be strong and of a good courage; be not afraid, neither be thou dismayed: for the LORD thy God is with thee whithersoever thou goest" (Joshua 1:9).

In August of 2007, my dad and I took a road trip together from Romeo, Michigan down to Tulsa, Oklahoma. We spent over 980 miles and two days together in a Midnight Blue Jeep Liberty. We are both relatively tall, so it was quite a squished ride! We listened to Christian music, sermons, and talked a lot on the way down. He was accompanying me to my first semester away at school and would fly back home after seeing me into my dorm.

My passage from Michigan to Oklahoma with my dad reminds me a great deal of how the Holy Spirit of God goes with us into new territories in our lives. We, like Joshua, may feel that we are on a terrifying journey. God had to tell Joshua four times in nine verses that He was going with Joshua and Joshua need not be afraid. God actually *commanded* Joshua not to fear, but to be strong, courageous, and to have a good attitude about walking into the unknown future. Joshua was called to take over where Moses left off – quite a daunting task! – and to do so, he would need to know that His God was going before and with him into this yet unconquered Promised Land. The Promise Land spiritually and legally belonged to the people of Israel, but the task of obtaining and securing it for the people was left to the leadership of Joshua upon Moses' passing.

There are times in our lives where we may feel God leading us to the impossible. Not only is the territory unfamiliar, but there are giants in the land we must face and conquer. During the time of Joshua, there were several tribes of giants, many of whom inhabited the land of Canaan. God was not unaware of this fact and certainly knew ahead of time which battles Joshua and the people of Israel were going to face. To properly prepare and equip his servant, Joshua, for what was ahead of him, God gave him only one piece of weaponry: the knowledge that "...the Lord thy God is with thee whithersoever thou goest". If God is calling you out into the ocean of the unknown, rest assured that He is with you as He was with Joshua and He will faithfully lead you into your Promised Land.

Today, I will not fear, but I will instead put my trust in the leading of the Lord, wherever He may take me.

DAY ELEVEN

"He that dwelleth in the secret place of the Most High shall abide under the shadow of the Almighty. I will say of the LORD, He is my refuge and my fortress: my God; in him will I trust. Surely he shall deliver thee from the snare of the fowler, and from the noisome pestilence. He shall cover thee with his feathers, and under his wings shalt thou trust: his truth shall be thy shield and buckler. Thou shalt not be afraid for the terror by night; nor for the arrow that flieth by day" (Psalm 91:1-5).

It was December and a cold, wet, snowy December at that. I was driving on my way back from work, only a few minutes from home. My parents and three younger brothers were watching television in the living room when suddenly our golden retriever began to bark at something on the back porch. My dad saw footprints. Someone had been peering through and had attempted to open the sliding glass door! I was just about to pull into the driveway when I noticed a white van parked a few feet down the road. As I parked and walked up to the house, I heard someone behind the front door. I went to open the door only to discover it was locked – something we were not accustomed to often doing. Immediately, the door swung open and I was greeted by my dad and two of my brothers, all three holding loaded shotguns aimed at my face!

To say I was scared at that moment was an understatement. That was the moment I became acquainted with the phrase "terror by night." I was instantly angry and afraid. How dare someone attempt to break into our home! Didn't they know Christians, people under the protection of Almighty God, lived here? They had no right! And, because they had no right, they were unable to carry out their plans against us.

God is well able to keep us safe – even from those who purpose to do us wrong. His Word declares that as we rest in Him, in the shelter and place of safety He provides in His presence, we are kept from all evil. That day, God used the readiness of my dad and brothers through the faithful and alert warning of our dog to ward off the would-be robbers – who were later caught at a break-in a neighborhood away from ours – and to safeguard our well-being and our possessions. God provides safety from every form of harm that would try to come against us. Beloved, take shelter in the protective covering of His shadow, in the secret place of His presence, and He will keep you safe from all harm.

Today, I will remain in the secret place of the Most High, taking refuge in His shadow, putting complete trust in His ability to keep me safe from all harm.

DAY TWELVE

"There is no fear in love; but perfect love casteth out fear: because fear hath torment. He that feareth is not made perfect in love" (1 John 4:18).

Having a baby is a lot of work! First, there are the nine months of growing and sustaining the little one. Then comes the task of bringing him or her into the world. I was all set to give birth to my second child, a little girl, when I hit some speed bumps in the road. I was due, but my body was not ready for her yet. Instead, I was experiencing high blood pressure because I was retaining so much water. The doctors decided to induce me. I went to the hospital with contractions, expecting to go into labor, and was told that I would have to do a Cesarean section the next morning. That was not what I wanted and I was scared to do a repeat C-section. Nonetheless, I went through with it. The first few days of recovery went smoothly. Then at a checkup, my blood pressure registered at a dangerously high level. I was readmitted to the hospital and told I was pre-eclamptic, in danger of having a stroke.

That night I spent in the ICU ward of the hospital was the single most terrifying night of my life. A nurse even came in to inform me that the medicine I was receiving through the IV could cause seizures or even death. What got me through was the love and prayers of many wonderful people. My sweet husband was next to me in the hospital. My mom was at my home taking care of my son and my dad was on the phone with me taking authority over the situation and rebuking fear while declaring I would live and not die. It was the love of God through His people that kept me from becoming paralyzed with fear. It was His love through my dad's reassuring prayers, my husband's presence at my side, my mom's faithfulness in watching my son, and so many others who had me on their heart and lifted me up before the Lord that conquered and dispelled the fear that was trying to dominate the situation. Perfect love entered into that hospital room with me and cast out fear, leaving me with perfect peace and a stabilized, lower blood pressure.

Whenever you are facing a terrifying situation and fear threatens to stop your heart, remember that the perfect love of the Lord eradicates fear because fear has torment and is not of Him. In His name, through His love, we have authority over fear and can rest in His perfect peace.

Today, I will let the perfect love of the Lord cast fear out of my heart and bring me peace in every situation I face.

DAY THIRTEEN

"Train up a child in the way he should go: and when he is old, he will not depart from it" (Proverbs 22:6).

I loved going to karate class every week. It was my coveted daddy-daughter time and I enjoyed every moment of it. Not only did I get to beat the daylights out of someone in sparring and emerge a mighty warrior from the fights, but my dad and I had a particular ritual we held to after every class: ice cream at the Swirly Top! A strawberry-dipped vanilla and chocolate swirled cone with sprinkles - that was my order. My dad's was not as fancy. His was just a simple cone, usually chocolate. I looked forward to this time with my dad every week.

That is why, when I got caught in a lie, I chose to take a few spankings instead of missing my karate night with my dad. I remember grabbing a few books to use as padding...which were quickly discovered and removed. Then, I did what every smart child would do as a Plan B - I tightened my little cheeks so tightly you could've bounced a brick off of them!

Although I still felt the sting of the wooden paddle on which my dad had engraved the Proverbs 22:6 reference, I felt something else that day, too. I felt my dad's pride in my choice. In fact, I remember him even bragging to my karate sensei that night how I had chosen to take a spanking over missing karate. My dad was not thrilled with the fact that I had lied, but he *was* impressed with what I chose to do about it. I took responsibility and received my punishment and then went on to enjoy the rest of my night pummeling kids in class and spending time with my daddy.

Many times in our Christian walks God desires to discipline us if we're willing to receive it. He does not do it in the form of a spanking like I got as a kid, but in other ways like pruning us from relationships or habits that keep us from becoming the person He designed us to become. Like a good father uses disciplinary actions to correct bad behavior and then brags on his child for making wise or mature choices, our Heavenly Father longs to train us up in the way He desires us to go. As we submit to His correction and guidance, not only will we grow and progress quicker in our development, we'll make Him proud in the process. And, who knows, maybe He'll even treat you to a cone at the Swirly Top on your date night with Daddy God.

Today, I will allow the Holy Spirit to train me in the way that I should go, submitting to His discipline and guidance.

DAY FOURTEEN

"Bless the LORD, O my soul: and all that is within me, bless his holy name. Bless the LORD, O my soul, and forget not all his benefits: Who forgiveth all thine iniquities; who healeth all thy diseases" (Psalm 103:1-3).

My mom had poop duty and my dad had puke duty when we were kids. If anyone soiled the bed, we called Mom. If we were retching in the bathroom, we hollered for Dad. And we never got confused on whom to call.

I can recall many a night where my dad was faithfully standing by, holding back my hair as I spilled the contents of my stomach. He was always so sweet, so compassionate – even in the middle of the night when I'm sure he was more than tempted to just walk away and let us kids deal with it ourselves. He didn't. He stayed right by our sides until we felt better.

God is able to do more than just holding back our hair while we get sick. He's able to actually remove sickness from our midst, to heal us. It's one of the many benefits we have as His children, to receive healing from Him. The Psalmist David commanded his soul not to forget all of the benefits of God and His manifest presence – and the very first thing he demanded he remember was that God first forgives and secondly heals us!

If there is any sickness, illness, disease, or infirmity in your life you're struggling against, here is a word for you: "…I am the Lord that healeth thee" (Exodus 15:2d). Remind yourself that you are forgiven and, as the righteousness of God in Christ Jesus (2 Corinthians 5:21), you are able to receive your healing from Him without any guilt or condemnation stealing it away.

Today, I will remember all of the many good things the Lord has done for me and the benefits of being His in Christ Jesus. I will allow His healing touch to remove from me all sickness, illness, disease, and infirmity so that I am made completely whole in Him.

DAY FIFTEEN

"But I keep under my body, and bring it into subjection: lest that by any means, when I have preached to others, I myself should be a castaway" (1 Corinthians 9:27).

Every morning at five o'clock, sometimes as early as 4 am, my dad's alarm would sound, rousing me from my sleep. Sharing the bedroom wall with his room meant that I could hear him rising from his slumber to head down to the garage for his morning workout routine. For quite a while, he would wake up daily to go running on the treadmill. He was beating his body into submission, demanding it to remain in health. I believe he will be as strong at eighty-five as he was at forty (Joshua 14:11).

My dad didn't just force his body to exercise physically through running. He also forced it to respond to spiritual training, that of fasting. My dad would often go on one-day, three-day, or even week-long liquid-only fasts just to spend time praying and seeking God. I believe it was this habit that eventually led to some significant spiritual breakthroughs for him.

God wants us to be in health and prosper even as our souls prosper (3 John 1:2). This means not only taking care of our physical bodies, but making sure not to neglect our souls – our minds, wills, and emotions - and our spirits in our exercising. Just as we can form diligent habits of hitting the gym on a routine basis, we need to engage in making wise choices emotionally and spending time fasting so we grow closer to and are positioned to receive answers and breakthroughs from God. Fasting has brought my dad to greater levels of maturity in his walk with the Lord and has ushered him into new realms of anointing and glory. If you are in a place where you need to break through to another level in your relationship with the Lord, you need answers to problems or solutions to situations around you, consider setting aside the silverware for some extra time in His presence, fasting before Him. Just as working out physically benefits the body, fasting benefits the spirit and helps bring forth His plan for our lives.

Today, I will seek the Lord through prayer and fasting, positioning myself to hear from Heaven so that I can be catapulted into the breakthroughs He has in store for me.

DAY SIXTEEN

"But the anointing which ye have received of him abideth in you, and ye need not that any man teach you: but as the same anointing teacheth you of all things, and is truth, and is no lie, and even as it hath taught you, ye shall abide in him" (1 John 2:27).

My dad has always been an inventor. As a man with several degrees and patented inventions, his mind is always going, going, going. The Lord has even awakened him in the middle of the night with ideas. He always carries a mini composition notebook in his shirt pocket to record new ideas throughout the day. My dad has stacks of mini composition notebooks filled with page after page of inventions the Lord has given him.

It was time spent with the Lord that brought about the ideas my dad is currently running with for his musical inventions. God gave him the name of the company, the product, and even gave him specific details of what materials to use and how to construct these items. In praying for my dad concerning these creations, the Lord has more than once used me to confirm to my dad that the answer he thought he stumbled upon was indeed an answer from Heaven.

I remember one particular conversation where I specified to my dad that the material he had just switched over to was the right material for that part he was working on. Another time, God gave me wisdom concerning the body design of what my dad was drawing up.

My dad knows a lot about guitars and musical equipment. I, however, know nothing. It was incredible to me that the Holy Spirit was able to impart to my dad the necessary information to further his project – even at times through me, a person with no understanding whatsoever of mechanics, electronics, and the like.

It is because my dad yielded to the leading of the Holy Spirit that he is where he is today, headed on the path to great financial success and freedom, making headlines while making a difference in the Kingdom of God. The Holy Spirit taught my dad what he needed to know to cause my dad to be successful in his entrepreneurship. In the same way, God is able to teach you and cause you to have supernatural knowledge for whatever ideas you are trying to piece together. As you honor Him and give Him a place in your life, He is able to make you of quick understanding (Isaiah 11:3) and bring supernatural solutions to what may seem like insurmountable challenges.

Today, I will seek the Lord and be open to His promptings, expecting Him to teach me things I need to know and to supply answers to problems I am facing.

DAY SEVENTEEN

"And the Lord spoke to Moses, saying: See, I have called by name Bezaleel the son of Uri, the son of Hur, of the tribe of Judah. And I have filled him with the spirit of God, in wisdom, and in understanding, and in knowledge, and in all manner of workmanship, to devise cunning works, to work in gold, and in silver, and in brass" (Exodus 31:1-4).

It is fascinating to me how God builds upon one experience after another to create the fulfillment of our destiny. It is so interesting to look back over my dad's life and see now how certain moments have culminated into his present reality. One of those particular moments was when my dad bought some woodworking equipment. I loved watching him use the scroll saw to make different plaques, ornaments, and pens, as well as decorative jewelry and pen boxes. I still have the very first thing he made, a slightly lopsided heart he cut out of a piece of oak.

Although my dad viewed his woodworking at the time as just a hobby, he learned the skill of how to fashion various beautiful three-dimensional objects from a plain block of wood. God has used my dad's engineering background and experience on the scroll saw to be able to see the end result and create musical masterpieces from raw materials. He has indeed gifted him in all manner of workmanship!

The Word says in Romans 11:29, "For the gifts and calling of

God are without repentance." The New International Version says they are "irrevocable." They are never taken away, but are always working for you to produce your future. Even when my dad was just playing around with a fun hobby, the gifts and calling of God were at work in his life to invent and design new creations, driving him forward to the moment when God would put on his heart the ideas for his new musical inventions and he would have the wherewithal to make it happen.

The knowledge my dad gained through woodworking over a decade ago has contributed to his success in current endeavors. It is probable that there are hobbies and interests you once enjoyed or currently are engaged in that are actually stepping stones into your future. There is no experience, good or bad, that goes wasted when God is in control of your destiny. Regardless of any "missed opportunity" or "wrong turn" you may have made in life, remember that He works "...all things together for the good of those who love God: those who are called according to His purpose (Romans 8:28)." He has designed you with gifts and talents He intends to use for His glory. Take a moment today to surrender them back into God's hands and seek His direction on how He plans to use them in your life.

Today, I will give my gifts and talents back to God, rededicating them to His purposes and allowing Him to use them to bring glory to His name.

DAY EIGHTEEN

"A man's gift maketh room for him, and bringeth him before great men" (Proverbs 18:16).

"Watch" was the name of their band. Rodney, Mike, Rick, and Steve were the other members. It was down in the basement of one of my dad's practices that I first picked up and sang into a microphone. It was down in that basement where I got to hear my dad jam with the guys. Now, years later, my dad has played acoustic, electric, and bass guitar for decades on the church worship team. I have been a worship director for a large church, have led worship overseas for crusade ministries, and have professional recordings of my music.

What started so long ago in a basement has led to both my dad and I using our talents to bring glory to the Lord. It was where he honed his skills and I learned I had skills. Over time, with much practice in our skill sets we have both become excellent musicians and love to worship the Lord with our musical abilities. Our gifts "made room" for us.

God longs to draw out of His people the giftings that are within so He can position them in various sectors of life to bring glory to His name. When you apply your heart to diligence and you develop the abilities you've been given, you will eventually find yourself at a place where you are using those talents and are fulfilled doing so.

Ask the Lord to show you today where your gifts have become dormant so they may be stirred up and fanned into flame once again. Ask Him to resurrect old passions that are part of your calling and to grant you open doors to use your abilities to serve Him.

Today, I will ask the Lord to show me opportunities I have to serve Him with my gifts.

DAY NINETEEN

"To every thing there is a season, and a time to every purpose under the heaven" (Ecclesiastes 3:1).

My dad is the King of Phases. He has always gone through seasons where he would become very interested in one thing or activity in particular and seem to focus the majority of his energy on that one item. One phase he went through that we all enjoyed was the Moon Pie phase. He would bring home multiple boxes at a time of Moon Pies. Some were chocolate, some vanilla, and several boxes were the banana-flavored pastries. They tasted great just out of the package, but were even better when microwaved for ten seconds. Needless to say, this phase didn't last very long because everyone kept getting into his stash!

Soon after the Moon Pies he went through another yummy phase, the malt powder phase. This was personally my favorite of his phases. He would stock up on jars of chocolate malt powder and have a few glasses each night. Eventually, my brothers and I drank enough of his supply that he stopped buying it and moved on to another phase - the exercise equipment phase.

After buying the desserts, he decided it was time to work out and invested in various pieces of workout equipment, spending hours at a time in the garage exercising. My brothers loved this phase and took full advantage of the home gym. It became a hangout for the guys and their friends and eventually my dad went back to another food phase - buying Perrier Water by the case. The boys and my mom didn't care much for Perrier Water, so my dad and I got to enjoy this one a little while longer.

My brothers also really enjoyed the guns and ammo, tools, and the riding toys phases. Later down the road my dad even got into making his own soda! My dad was constantly interested in something new and loading up on whatever it was.

Just like my dad would often go through phases of interests, from junk food to exercising, we go through phases in life called 'seasons.' These seasons may last a moment or several years, but they are there to teach us Kingdom principles, such as sowing and reaping or planting and harvesting. The Bible says, "While the earth remaineth, seedtime, and harvest, and cold and heat, and summer and winter, and day and night shall not cease" (Genesis 8:22). Every season in nature has its appointed time and purpose.

Each season of life God brings you through also has designated time and purpose. There may be times of crying and times of laughing, times to hold your peace and times to speak, times to hold close, and times to let go. No one season lasts forever; seasons are designed to change. If everything is going your way, praise God and keep going. If you are in a season of your life where things are tough, hang in there, they will get better. Whatever season you find yourself in today, know that it is temporary, subject to change, just like my dad and his phases.

Today, I will take heart and know that my season is about to change for my good.

DAY TWENTY

"And when he had removed him, he raised up unto them David to be their king; to whom also he gave their testimony, and said, I have found David the son of Jesse, a man after mine own heart, which shall fulfill all my will" (Acts 13:22).

A memory I cherish of my dad is a moment that happened fairly recently in a small local church, Rochester First Assembly of God. My dad was prayerfully seeking to leave the church he had attended for quite some time and had joined me at the church my husband and I called 'home.' It was there in the presence of God in the midst of worship that I saw my dad moved by the power of the Holy Spirit. He cried. He rejoiced. He praised. He worshiped. He even began to pray in the Spirit, something he at that time was not in the habit of often doing. He turned to me in that service and said that he knew the Spirit of God was in that place and that was where he was supposed to be. It was beautiful to see my dad's heart toward the Lord.

That's something that I love about my dad: his heart. He strives to be sensitive to the leading of the Holy Spirit and live a life that is pleasing to God. When I think of King David, whom God called a "man after mine own heart," I think of my dad and his reverent heart of worship. My dad understands what it is to "worship in spirit and in truth" (John 4:24).

God desires people who will give themselves entirely to Him, to lose themselves in Him. He said of King David that he was a man who would do the will of God. As Believers, we need to be known around the world as a people who are after God's heart. We need to be found pursuing His heart and the things that matter to Him. We need our own hearts transformed so we replicate His character within them. We need to be known as people who desire to do His will.

Today, I will allow my heart to be softened in His presence so that I can become a person after His own heart.

DAY TWENTY-ONE

"Confess your faults one to another, and pray one for another, that ye may be healed. The effectual fervent prayer of a righteous man availeth much" (James 5:16).

Growing up, I had the privilege of having a wonderful, godly grandmother, my dad's mom, Emma Louise. She was a Bible school teacher who often volunteered in various ministries at her church. Most of all, she was a woman of the Word. I remember her sitting on the bed pouring over the Bible, studying and preparing to teach the Scriptures. Many times when I would spend the night, I would accompany her to church, sometimes joining in on her classes, and sit next to her on the old wooden pews at Dequindre Road Baptist Church. Brother Brink's sermons were often over my head at such a young age, but my grandma was glued to every word. I believe it was from her example that my dad developed his love of the Lord and the things of God. He followed in her footsteps and became a man of the Word and a man of prayer.

One thing I admire about my dad is his diligence. He spends every morning and every evening in the Word and prayer before the Lord for an hour. He has faithfully kept this habit for over 30 years. I know where I will find him in another 30: in the chair next to his bed, reading His Bible and lifting up his voice to God bright and early in the morning when he first wakes up and again late at night as the last thing he does before he closes his eyes.

I have no doubt that the time my dad has spent reading his Bible and praying has been productive. I have seen miracles, breakthroughs, salvations, and healings occur as a direct result of my dad's persistence in prayer. I have heard him, when he thought no one was around, crying out before the Lord, pouring his heart out to the Father on behalf of his family, pastors, and people he loves. What my dad has done in secret has brought incredible answers to prayer out into the open and has "availed much."

Whether you start with five minutes or an hour, setting aside time throughout your day to seek the Lord in prayer will accomplish so much in so many areas of your life. Being diligent and passionate – fervent in your prayer life – can turn situations around for the better while drawing you into a closer relationship with the Father.

Today, I will purpose to develop a deeper, more meaningful prayer life and prepare for answers to those prayers.

DAY TWENTY-TWO

"But ye, beloved, building up yourselves on your most holy faith, praying in the Holy Ghost" (Jude 20).

What initially began as an hour every morning and evening in prayer in his native English tongue went on to evolve into something even more powerful: praying in the Spirit. When my dad learned the power of praying in the Holy Ghost, or in tongues, he grabbed ahold of it and has never been the same since. He started by purposing to pray for about ten minutes a day, then that grew to an hour, and now he prays close to three hours a day in his heavenly language.

What my dad has tapped into is what Jude calls "building up yourself on your most holy faith." In Ephesians 6:10 we are told to be "...strong in the Lord and the power of His might." I believe part of how we strengthen ourselves in Him is through praying in the Spirit to build ourselves up.

In Greek, the word "build" refers to an actual building, such as a house. The picture created by the verbiage is that praying in tongues causes us to add to ourselves the way a contractor would erect a home. We first lay the foundation, then put up the framework for the walls, and after all the work is done within the home, we add the roof. In the same way that a house is constructed from the bottom up, praying in our heavenly language lays a spiritual foundation and then builds upon it, furnishing us with good works and godly character.

Praying in the Holy Spirit bypasses the understanding of the mind and allows us to pray perfect prayers. Praying perfect prayers enables us to receive perfect answers. Paul calls this "speaking mysteries" unto God in 1 Corinthians 14:2. It is a weapon both offensive and defensive in our armory. Because it supersedes the understanding, the influence of our minds, wills, and emotions does not interfere with what we are praying. It is also not understood by the devil and allows us to agree with God for His perfect will in a situation without exposing God's plans to the enemy, keeping him from strategizing against what the Lord is bringing to pass.

If you do not have a spiritual prayer language yet, but already know Jesus as your Savior, only ask the Lord and then open your mouth by faith and He will fill it with a heavenly language as you are baptized in the Holy Spirit. Luke 11:13 says, "If ye then, being evil, know how to give good gifts unto your children: how much more shall your heavenly Father give the Holy Spirit to them that ask him?" He is eager to impart this gift to you so you can begin to pray His perfect will.

Today, I will be filled with the Spirit and speak in other tongues, agreeing with God for His perfect will to come to pass in my life.

DAY TWENTY-THREE

"But my God shall supply all your need according to his riches in glory by Christ Jesus" (Philippians 4:19).

God always provides. Even when it doesn't look like it's possible, He is the God of the impossible and there will be provision. Isaiah 43:19 goes as far as to say that where there is nothing, God will create something: in a dry and parched land, He will create streams of water! Where there is no path to get to where you need to go, He will create a pathway in the wilderness for you.

I experienced this provision in 2008 when I was preparing for a mission trip with Dominic Russo Ministries. I had been asked to help lead worship in Spanish for the women's conference and crusades, as well as interpret for the teams going to the Dominican Republic. I did my best to fundraise, and my last attempt to raise the final funds I needed was a garage sale. All was going well until it rained unexpectedly and most of what I was selling was ruined by the downpour. The deadline was only a day or two away and the situation looked utterly hopeless. There was no way I would be able to come up with the remaining amount without a miracle.

That's when the Lord spoke to my dad and laid it on his heart to make up the difference so that I could attend the mission trip. My dad, a cheerful giver and faithful to obey, obliged and supplied the last of the finances I needed to go to the Dominican Republic.

Because of my dad's obedience, he shares in the harvest of souls won and the seeds planted in the hearts of over 30,000 people who heard about the Lord because of that mission trip. Through his generosity, blind eyes were opened, demons were cast out, and natives in little huts in remote villages were blessed by worship in their own language. God blessed my faith and allowed my dad to partner with what He was doing to provide and my dad will share for eternity in that reward.

If God needs to get something to you and you are standing in faith for Him to provide, rest assured that He will use even your enemies to get the blessing to you if needed. He did that for the people in 2 Kings Chapter 7. In the matter of one day, they went from starving as an entire city to abundant surplus the very next morning. The Lord is well able to meet your needs and is ready to do so for you today.

Today, I will stand in faith, confident that God is even now meeting my needs through whatever means possible.

DAY TWENTY-FOUR

"Delight thyself also in the Lord: and he shall give thee the desires of thine heart" (Psalm 37:4).

Everyone has experienced rough seasons in their lives and I know I've certainly encountered some in my own. There is one season in particular that stands out to me where I was struggling financially. I was unemployed and had sent out over a hundred resumes...to be met with absolutely no response. Even McDonald's was not interested in hiring me. I was overqualified for simple positions, underqualified for higher-paying positions, and the positions for which I was well-suited were overstaffed. I was having trouble making ends meet and even got low on groceries.

That's when my dad stepped in and offered to help. He called me from work and asked me what groceries I needed. I gave him a list of organic, non-GMO foods I considered to be essential and then added, "Oh, and tomatoes!" There was something that sounded so divine about a vine-ripened tomato with sea salt. It was calling me. And I was too broke to answer. My dad initially told me that tomatoes weren't important and would be too expensive from Trader Joe's. When he showed up at my door that afternoon, however, at the top of the bag were four huge vine-ripened beefsteak tomatoes. I cried.

My dad went beyond just helping meet a need. He met a desire.

It wasn't necessary that he grab tomatoes – cereal and milk would've sufficed. He, a good dad and a generous giver, decided that it was worth the few extra dollars to minister love to me and grant me what was at that moment a desire of my heart, my tomatoes. I don't know that my dad ever realized the impact that had on me. It was such a small act of kindness and only a few dollars of expense to him.

What he taught me at that moment, however, is of infinite worth. God longs to give us the desires of our heart – even desires as trivial as tomatoes. Even when we are at our lowest and surviving is our most important goal, God longs to go a step beyond. He not only wants to meet our needs, but He also wants to bless us with our desires. He is a good Father and loves to see His children happy, fulfilled, and enjoying His good gifts. Take a moment today to recognize Him in the little things and don't be afraid to ask for something that you may consider insignificant. He yearns for us to know Him intimately as Provider, even of tomatoes.

Today, I will ask God for even the small things on my heart that matter to me and watch Him joyfully provide as only a good Father can.

DAY TWENTY-FIVE

"Every good gift and every perfect gift is from above, and comes down from the Father of lights, with whom there is no variableness, neither shadow of turning" (James 1:17).

One of the ways my dad receives love is through words of affirmation. Another love language of his is physical touch. A primary way he gives love to others, however, is through gift-giving. I remember being a young girl when my dad would have to travel overseas to look after the affairs of Chrysler in certain engineering areas. He went once to Amsterdam and brought back gifts of flavored chocolate. My favorite was the orange-infused chocolate. Gifts he brought home from another trip were bracelets for my mom and me. It was exciting to see what my daddy would bring back for us. We always looked forward to when he would come home from abroad.

In our home, Christmas was my mom's territory. She WAS Santa. She would very carefully and lovingly pick out an abundance of fantastic presents that we all enjoyed. My dad would lounge on the couch while we all opened our gifts. Then at the very end, he would bring out a special gift he had picked out himself for us.

One particular Christmas, he bought me exotic soaps made in Chile with different herbs and essential oils. Along with that was a Japanese language book for me to study. No matter what my dad got us, they were always very thoughtful gifts that showed how well he knew us.

God is the Ultimate Giver and He loves to bless us. His gifts, like my dad's, show how well He knows us. His gifts do not always come packaged with ribbons and bows, or are reserved only for the holidays. His gifts come in a variety of shapes and sizes every day. If He woke you up today, that is a gift! If you are able to move, breathe, and accomplish tasks on your own, that is a gift! Every smile, every rainbow in the sky, every moment of silence in an otherwise chaotic day – those are all gifts He gives us. Sometimes, gifts come in the form of friendship, a kind and encouraging word, a close parking spot when you're in a hurry, a sale at the grocery store when you're on a tight budget, another register opening up when you've been standing in a long line, a rerun of a favorite movie airing on tv after a long day at work, or a word of prophecy when you're about to give up believing for your miracle. All of these are gifts. Take a moment today to recognize the gifts you've been given and give Him thanks.

Today, I will choose an attitude of gratitude and take the time to count my blessings.

DAY TWENTY-SIX

"The steps of a good man are ordered by the Lord: and he delighteth in his way" (Psalm 37:23).

I knew that I knew that I knew that I knew that I was going to be getting married soon. The problem was that I didn't know to whom! The Lord had laid it on my heart to get ready. I was about to be getting married - and sooner than I expected. It was less than three months from when He spoke that word to my heart that I was standing on Kailua Beach in my beautiful home state of Hawaii, holding hands and exchanging vows with my best friend and now beloved husband, Robert.

My parents initially thought I was nuts when I called to announce to them God had told me I was going to be celebrating my wedding soon. They believed me, but just weren't sure how God was going to bring it to pass since I wasn't even dating anyone at the time. My dad felt that word resonated as truth within his spirit and he began to pray for me that God would work things out for His perfect will to be done in that area. In what seemed like no time at all, I was calling my dad to tell him that my best friend and I realized we loved each other as much more than just friends and we went from best friends to engaged in one day. We didn't even date until after we were betrothed.

Thirty-eight days after we got engaged, we got married. My

parents flew out to Hawaii for an incredible week together with us before the big day. We had so many wonderful times together showing them our favorite places, teaching them Hawaiian phrases, and even introducing them to ethnic Hawaiian foods at a Hawaiian restaurant. Everything was going smoothly and we were all set for a beautiful, intimate wedding. Everything was in place. Everything except for my wedding ring.

I so fondly cherish this memory of my dad and my husband going together to pick out my wedding ring. They went to a few different stores in search for the perfect ring and finally, after praying for the right ring they were led straight to it at a store about to close. They came back to the hotel where my parents were staying with looks of satisfaction on their faces. They had had a mission, and it had been accomplished.

Just as my husband and father both delighted in such an important detail of the wedding, our Heavenly Father delights in all the little details of our lives, big and small. He has every step ordered, or purposed, for us to walk in and He takes such joy in each aspect of our lives. He always knows exactly what is up ahead and can lead us straight to the very best deals, answers to problems, and greatest blessings if we are faithful to follow His leading.

Today, I will walk in the steps God has ordained for me and watch His favor be poured out on my life as I include him in the details of it.

DAY TWENTY-SEVEN

"Thou art good, and doest good; teach me thy statutes" (Psalm 119:68).

My wedding in Hawaii was nothing short of a miracle. Not only had God told me I was going to get married soon when there was no man in my life, but my parents lived in Michigan and didn't have the finances to fly out for the wedding. I had wanted to get married on Kailua Beach, the place where I had spent so incredible many daddy-daughter dates with God. I would go every Tuesday to spend the entire day in His presence. I would bring my Bible with me and sometimes journal. More times than not, He would call me out into the deep parts of the ocean, about a mile past the swim zone. There I would just commune in deep fellowship with Him, worshipping as I swam and enjoyed the beauty and majesty of His creation. I craved that time with Him and looked forward to it every week.

The problem with getting married on Kailua Beach, other than pulling a permit, is that it has unfortunately become a bit of a tourist trap and is often overcrowded. I wanted a quiet, intimate wedding with no one else around. Aside from tourists in rented kayaks, Kailua Beach is a great spot to windsurf and is usually cluttered with the sails and boards of windsurfers. I knew that was where I had to get married. It was the perfect place for my Heavenly Husband to give me over to my earthly husband. I just didn't know how it was going to happen the way I wanted. All I could do was pray.

I prayed and asked God that it would rain, that there would be terrible weather all day in Kailua until just before the wedding so that there would be no one on the beach. I prayed God would make a way for my parents to be there with me. I also wanted to have my reception dinner at the Kalapawai Café, another place near the beach that was significant to me which was completely booked that evening. I didn't have a photographer for my wedding, either and was just hoping the camera on my archaic flip phone would suffice.

In one amazing miracle after another, God showered His goodness on my special day. The Lord provided, as He always does, and my mom and dad were able to join us for our special day. My daddy wouldn't take 'no' for an answer when it came to walking his only little girl down the aisle, sandy as it was. When we arrived in Kailua that afternoon, the sun was just beginning to peek out from behind a cloud. It had stormed with cold, hard, driving rain all day until the hour of my wedding. There were only five other people on the entire several-mile stretch of beach, something I had never seen before or since. My beautiful actress friend, a fellow author and artist, Faith Fay, blessed us unexpectedly with her professional photography skills as a gift to us at our wedding. Then, she went a step further and used her fame as an actress to get special permission for a closed section of the Kalapawai Café to be opened for us to enjoy our reception dinner.

In one situation after another, God's goodness and favor opened doors for my wedding to be absolutely perfect. God is good and all He is capable of doing is good and good only. He is just looking for people who will believe He is good and expect His goodness to be made manifest in their lives. Dare to believe He has goodness in store for you and watch Him pour it out upon you.

Today, I will experience the goodness God has in store for me and give Him the glory for His great goodness toward me.

DAY TWENTY-EIGHT

"And the scripture was fulfilled which saith, Abraham believed God, and it was imputed unto him for righteousness: and he was called the Friend of God" (James 2:23).

Now that I am an adult, I am able to enjoy the benefit of friendship with a godly father. As a kid, I never thought my parents would become my friends. I was never able to conceive the idea of having a relationship where we would be able to exchange thoughts, ideas, and even mutually give and receive advice from each other as equals in the faith. Now, I am able to say both of my parents are counted among my closest friends.

This season with my dad is truly my most favorite, being able to appreciate his company and fellowship on a deeper level with him. We get lost in conversation for an hour or more on the phone every time we call to chat, and we stay up late for several hours talking in person. We have gone on daddy-daughter dates, went through scientific video curriculums and listened to sermons together, created music with one another, and just enjoyed spending quality time together. I have come to relish his wisdom and experience and he has come to value my insight and discernment. We have a balanced, healthy, mutually participatory relationship that has created a deep friendship between us. For this, I am truly grateful.

The friendship for which I am most grateful is the one I have with my Heavenly Father. There truly is no better friend than Jesus and no closer a helper and advocate than the Holy Spirit. In James 2:23, the Bible says that God called His servant, Abraham, His friend. Imagine, the Creator of the universe, the One who knows everything there is to know, is known as the All-Sufficient One because He has need of nothing chose to call a man, a created being who can do nothing on his own, His friend. In Genesis 18:17, God actually seeks Abraham's input on a decision He's about to make and allows Abraham to influence the outcome of God's plan. Genesis 32:28 calls this "power with God." The Living Bible says in Psalm 25:14, "Friendship with God is reserved for those who reverence him. With them alone he shares the secrets of his promises." We have been given the weighty responsibility and remarkable privilege of influence with God through friendship with Him. The Lord longs to fellowship with us and to know us intimately, as more than just servants of the Most High. He longs to know and trust us as His very best friend.

Today, I will purpose to develop a deeper relationship with the Lord, allowing Him to know me intimately and to count me among His friends.

DAY TWENTY-NINE

"Not forsaking the assembling of ourselves together, as the manner of some is; but exhorting one another: and so much the more, as ye see the day approaching" (Hebrews 10:25).

Now that I am able to enjoy fellowship with my dad, we have such a rich, deep relationship. Our friendship revolves primarily around our faith in God. We spend so much time building each other up, admonishing and encouraging each other, praying for one another, discussing the Bible, and sharing Kingdom principles we're learning. My dad and I have become the "iron sharpening iron" mentioned in Proverbs 27:17. We keep each other from becoming lackadaisical in our walks with the Lord. We inspire each other to stand in faith and keep on standing even when situations look impossible and we feel hopelessness creeping in. We challenge one another to believe for greater and to go from faith to faith and glory to glory, to continually press in for greater revelations and manifestations of Jesus in our lives.

Even though we don't live close anymore – we're several states away at the moment – my dad and I still make it a point to set aside time to assemble through phone calls and FaceTime to exhort each other. In his personal life, as well as in my own, we also gather together locally within our churches with other members of the Body of Christ for the purpose of reinforcing each other in the faith. There

57

have been countless times where a word spoken from the pulpit or another congregant has been the exact word we needed to hear to spark our faith, as an answer to prayer or to help us recalibrate in our daily lives.

In this way, we mimic the root systems of Redwood trees that intertwine together and keep each other standing. Even when a Redwood has died or is decaying, it remains standing because of the extensive network of intertwined roots, giving it strength from surrounding trees. This is the type of assembling together written about in the Bible, coming together with fellow like-minded believers who help you stand when you've done everything you can to keep standing. They become just as near and dear to you as your own family. They *are* family, actually, the Family of God.

If you don't have relatives close to you or people in your life who can uplift, challenge, and encourage you in the faith, ask the Lord to lead you to the right church and individuals. It is so important to develop relationships that spur you on and help strengthen you in the faith.

Today, I will recognize the "Redwoods" with which God has surrounded me and join my heart together with theirs in fellowship in Christ.

DAY THIRTY

"And they rose early in the morning, and went forth into the wilderness of Tekoa: and as they went forth, Jehoshaphat stood and said, Hear me, O Judah, and ye inhabitants of Jerusalem; Believe in the Lord your God, so shall ye be established; believe his prophets, so shall ye prosper." (2 Chronicles 20:20).

Many times people get stuck in a mindset that limits God and keeps Him in a box. My dad grew up hearing about the abilities of the Lord and the pertinence of His Word as the authority in our lives through a certain denominational lens. My dad has since expanded his expectations of the Lord and has a much more developed, mature faith in the power of the Word. As a result of realizing the power to create our destiny through the words we speak, good or bad, and the role the Scriptures play in producing the promises of God in our lives, my dad is diligent to watch what he says and whom he allows to influence his thinking.

Consequently, he has surrounded himself with faith-filled teachings by ministers such as Keith Moore, Kenneth Copeland, Jesse Duplantis, Jerry Savelle, Richard Crisco, and many others. He understands the value of the Word of God coming through these anointed men of God and how to recognize a prophet of the Lord from a false prophet, someone who is not authorized by God to speak words on His behalf, someone who is deceived and seeks to deceive others. My dad honors these God-appointed men as the oracles of the Lord and has even traveled states away to be in their presence just to experience the anointing of the Lord on them as they deliver His Word to His people.

My dad traveled to Ohio to see and shake hands with the man he considers to be his father in the faith, Brother Keith Moore. He said it was such an honor for him to be in the same building as him, and to sit under the anointing God has placed on this prophet of the Lord. Because he believes the Lord, my dad is established. Because he believes the prophets God has raised up for this hour in the Body of Christ, my dad prospers. This is key to success as a believer, recognizing and honoring the ministers God has appointed for this season on His timeline. God designed us to need Him and to need each other. He actually causes us to prosper when we honor the people He has placed as biblically prophetic authorities in our lives. Matthew 10:41 says that there is even a reward for honoring a prophet as the prophet of the Lord.

Today, I will honor the prophets of God and heed their words, believing to prosper and share in their reward.

DAY THIRTY-ONE

"A good man leaveth an inheritance to his children's children: and the wealth of the sinner is laid up for the just" (Proverbs 13:22).

I will forever remember February 2, 2012, and September 5, 2015. Those are the dates the Lord blessed me with my two beautiful children, a precious little boy, and a precious little girl. My dad was able to be present at the birth of his first grandson and soon will meet his first granddaughter. I will never forget the look on his face as he held my son in his arms. It was partly a comical, "I don't know what to do with something so small," look. And it was definitely the look of someone who recognized God had just added a blessing to our family.

My dad has grown and developed from a great parent into a wonderful grandpa. He is an absolute goofball when playing with my little boy. The louder the toy, the more fun it is – for both of them! And they have a blast tickling each other, playing guitar and singing together, and just spending time enjoying the unique relationship they have together. He is adored and admired, missed when he's not around, and enjoyed when he is. Papa is his superhero and role model.

My dad modeled a godly lifestyle to his children as we grew up in his household and now he continues to demonstrate a faith-filled life to his grandchildren. He will not only leave a physical inheritance of vast wealth to his grandbabies, but he will also leave them with a rich legacy of godliness. As they grow, they will learn from him, as my brothers and I did, how to walk by faith, believe for and receive the "impossible," and to develop a mature friendship and deep intimacy with the Lord. He has built his life upon the Rock and will give to his grandchildren a foundation they can build upon. His ceiling will become their floor and they will build for future generations of their own. This is the inheritance the godly leave their grandchildren as mentioned in Proverbs 13:22, a lifetime of serving Jesus and living Christ-like before them, teaching them to emulate Him and do the same.

Today, I will build with diligence the foundation for my grandchildren, for those who come behind me, and will purpose to live a life worth following.

PRAYER OF SALVATION

If you are not sure of your eternal destination and would like to make Jesus your Lord and Savior so that you, too, may enjoy a lifetime here on earth and eternity in His presence, pray the following prayer aloud and with your whole heart:

> "Father, I know that I have broken Your laws and have sinned. My sins have separated me from You and I acknowledge that believing in and receiving Jesus as my Lord and Savior is the only way to be reconciled with You. I believe Your Son, Jesus Christ, who is fully God and fully man, was born of a virgin, lived a sinless and holy life, died for my sins, was resurrected from the dead, is alive today and forevermore, and hears me when I pray. I repent of my sins and receive Your forgiveness right now. I invite Jesus to become the Lord of my life, to rule and reign in my heart, from this day forward, for all of eternity. Thank You for filling me now with and baptizing me in Your Holy Spirit. I receive Your gift of a Heavenly prayer language. I thank You for all You have done for me and for helping me to do Your will for the rest of my life. In Jesus' precious, mighty name I pray. Amen."

ABOUT THE AUTHOR

Kelly Valencia-Aiken is an artist, author, entrepreneur, singer, songwriter, teacher, and worship leader. She is the wife of an incredible husband and mommy of two wonderful children. She and her husband, Robert, have a passion to see Christians arise as the Bride of Christ, ruling and reigning in this life, making the kingdoms of this world the kingdoms of Jesus Christ. They work together to help Believers recognize and fulfill their God-given assignments. Although they currently reside in Colorado, Hawaii is home to this family that loves worshiping Jesus. She and her husband are looking forward to many, many more years of serving the Lord together in business and ministry and raising their children to do the same. To contact Robert and Kelly for ministry or speaking engagements, questions, or comments, please write to: LittleMsWordsmith@gmail.com.

Made in the USA
Charleston, SC
08 November 2015